Dec 2018

Dear Cindi,

I know you have been through a lot this year. managing children, husband, + hospital. Wish I had been able to help more. Just can't get around like I use to. Thought this book might help. I know we have our difference but please know that I love you, pray for you, + marvel at the job you do every day. Merry Christmas + Love you all,

Giggy

Presented to:

Cindi Dexon

Gregory
From:

_____

Date:

Christmas 2018

Jesus Calling®

50 Devotions for

Peace

Sarah Young

THOMAS NELSON
Since 1798

Published in Nashville, Tennessee, by Thomas Nelson. Thomas Nelson is a registered trademark of HarperCollins Christian Publishing, Inc.

Unless otherwise noted, Scripture quotations are taken from the Holy Bible, New International Version®, niv®. Copyright © 1973, 1978, 1984 by Biblica, Inc.® Used by permission of Zondervan. All rights reserved worldwide. www.zondervan.com. The "niv" and "New International Version" are trademarks registered in the United States Patent and Trademark Office by Biblica, Inc.®

Scripture quotations marked amp are from the Amplified® Bible. Copyright © 1954, 1958, 1962, 1964, 1965, 1987 by The Lockman Foundation. Used by permission. (www.Lockman.org)

Scripture quotations marked esv are from the esv® Bible (The Holy Bible, English Standard Version®). Copyright © 2001 by Crossway, a publishing ministry of Good News Publishers. Used by permission. All rights reserved.

Scripture quotations marked kjv are from the King James Version. Public domain.

Scripture quotations marked THE MESSAGE are from *The Message*. Copyright © by Eugene H. Peterson 1993, 1994, 1995, 1996, 2000, 2001, 2002. Used by permission of Tyndale House Publishers, Inc.

Scripture quotations marked nasb are from New American Standard Bible®. Copyright © 1960, 1962, 1963, 1968, 1971, 1972, 1973, 1975, 1977, 1995 by The Lockman Foundation. Used by permission. (www.Lockman.org)

Scripture quotations marked nkjv are from the New King James Version®. © 1982 by Thomas Nelson. Used by permission. All rights reserved.

Any Internet addresses, phone numbers, or company or product information printed in this book are offered as a resource and are not intended in any way to be or to imply an endorsement by Thomas Nelson, nor does Thomas Nelson vouch for the existence, content, or services of these sites, phone numbers, companies, or products beyond the life of this book.

ISBN 978-1-4003-1091-3

The Library of Congress has cataloged the earlier edition as follows:

Young, Sarah, 1946–
Jesus Calling / by Sarah Young.
p. cm.
ISBN 978-1-59145-188-4 (hardcover)
1. Devotional calendars. 2. Devotional literature, English. I. Title.
BV4811.Y675 2004
242'.2—dc22   2044005474

Printed in China

18 19 20 21 22 TIMS 5 4 3

INTRODUCTION

Now may the Lord of peace himself give
you peace at all times and in every way.

—2 THESSALONIANS 3:16

In many parts of the world, Christians seem to be searching for a deeper experience of Jesus' Presence and Peace. The devotions that follow address that felt need.

I have written from the perspective of Jesus speaking, to help readers feel more personally connected with Him. So the first person singular ("I," "Me," "My," "Mine") always refers to Christ; "you" refers to you, the reader. The devotions in this book are meant to be read slowly, preferably in a quiet place—with your Bible open. The Bible is the only infallible, inerrant Word of God, and I endeavor to keep my writings consistent with that unchanging standard. After each daily reading, I have included Scripture references. Words from the Scriptures (some paraphrased, some quoted) are indicated in italics.

Jesus knows each of us intimately, and He meets us right where we are—in the midst of our many needs. May you enjoy His Presence and His Peace in ever-increasing measure.

Sarah Young

REFRESH YOURSELF in the Peace of My Presence. This Peace can be your portion at all times and in all circumstances. Learn to *hide in the secret of My Presence*, even as you carry out your duties in the world. I am both with you and within you. I go before you to open up the way, and I also walk alongside you. There could never be another companion as devoted as I am.

Because I am your constant Companion, there should be a lightness to your step that is observable to others. Do not be weighed down with problems and unresolved issues, for I am your burden-bearer. In the world you have trials and distress, but don't let them get you down. *I have conquered the world and deprived it of power to harm you.* In Me you may have confident Peace.

PSALM 31:19–20 NASB; JOHN 16:33 AMP

"I have told you these things, so that in Me you may have [perfect] *peace* and confidence. In the world you have tribulation and trials and distress and frustration; but be of good cheer [take courage; be *confident*, certain, undaunted]! For I have overcome the world. [I have deprived it of *power* to harm you and have conquered it for you.]"

—JOHN 16:33 AMP

LET ME BLESS YOU with My grace and Peace. Open your heart and mind to receive all that I have for you. Do not be ashamed of your emptiness. Instead, view it as the optimal condition for being filled with My Peace.

It is easy to touch up your outward appearance, to look as if you have it all together. Your attempts to look good can fool most people. But I see straight through you, into the depths of your being. There is no place for pretense in your relationship with Me. Rejoice in the relief of being fully understood. Talk with Me about your struggles and feelings of inadequacy. Little by little, I will transform your weaknesses into strengths. Remember that your relationship with Me is saturated in grace. Therefore, *nothing that you do or don't do can separate you from My Presence.*

1 SAMUEL 16:7; ROMANS 8:38–39

But the LORD said to Samuel,

"Do not *consider* his

appearance or his height, for

I have rejected him. The LORD

does not look at the things

man looks at. Man looks at the

outward appearance, but the

LORD looks at the *heart*."

—1 SAMUEL 16:7

MY FACE IS SHINING UPON YOU, beaming out *Peace that transcends understanding.* You are surrounded by a sea of problems, but you are face to Face with Me, your Peace. As long as you focus on Me, you are safe. If you gaze too long at the myriad problems around you, you will sink under the weight of your burdens. When you start to sink, simply call out, "Help me, Jesus!" and I will lift you up.

The closer you live to Me, the safer you are. Circumstances around you are undulating, and there are treacherous-looking waves in the distance. *Fix your eyes on Me,* the One who never changes. By the time those waves reach you, they will have shrunk to proportions of My design. I am always beside you, helping you face *today's* waves. The future is a phantom, seeking to spook you. Laugh at the future! Stay close to Me.

PHILIPPIANS 4:7; MATTHEW 14:29–30; HEBREWS 12:2

And the peace of God, which *transcends* all understanding, will guard your *hearts* and your minds in Christ Jesus.

—Philippians 4:7

COME TO ME, and rest in My loving Presence. You know that this day will bring difficulties, and you are trying to think your way through those trials. As you anticipate what is ahead of you, you forget that *I am with you*—now and always. Rehearsing your troubles results in experiencing them many times, whereas you are meant to go through them only when they actually occur. Do not multiply your suffering in this way! Instead, come to Me, and relax in My Peace. I will strengthen you and prepare you for this day, transforming your fear into confident trust.

MATTHEW 11:28–30; JOSHUA 1:5, 9

"Come to me, all you who are
weary and burdened, and I
will give you *rest*. Take
my yoke upon you and learn
from me, for I am gentle and
humble in heart, and
you will find rest for your
souls. For my yoke is easy and
my burden is *light*."

—MATTHEW 11:28–30

SEEK MY FACE, and you will find more than you ever dreamed possible. *Let Me displace worry at the center of your being.* I am like a supersaturated cloud, showering Peace into the pool of your mind. My Nature is to bless. Your nature is to receive with thanksgiving. This is a true fit, designed before the foundation of the world. Glorify Me by receiving My blessings gratefully.

I am the goal of all your searching. *When you seek Me, you find Me* and are satisfied. When lesser goals capture your attention, I fade into the background of your life. I am still there, watching and waiting, but you function as if you were alone. Actually, My Light shines on every situation you will ever face. Live radiantly by expanding your focus to include Me in all your moments. Let nothing dampen your search for Me.

PSALM 27:8 NKJV; PHILIPPIANS 4:7 THE MESSAGE;
JEREMIAH 29:13

"You will

seek me

and find me

when you seek me

with all your

heart."

—Jeremiah 29:13

"No one will be able to stand up against you all the days of your life. As I was with Moses, so I will be with you; I will never leave you nor forsake you. . . . Have I not commanded you? Be strong and courageous. Do not be terrified; do not be discouraged, for the LORD your God will be with you wherever you go."

—Joshua 1:5, 9

MY PEACE is the treasure of treasures: *the pearl of great price*. It is an exquisitely costly gift, for both the Giver and the receiver. I purchased this Peace for you with My blood. You receive this gift by trusting Me in the midst of life's storms. If you have the world's peace—everything going your way—you don't seek My unfathomable Peace. Thank Me when things do not go your way, because spiritual blessings come wrapped in trials. Adverse circumstances are normal in a fallen world. Expect them each day. Rejoice in the face of hardship, *for I have overcome the world*.

MATTHEW 13:46 NKJV; JAMES 1:2–3; JOHN 16:33 ESV

Consider it pure *joy*,

my brothers, whenever you

face trials of many kinds,

because you know that the

testing of your *faith*

develops perseverance.

—JAMES 1:2-3

BRING ME YOUR WEAKNESS, and receive My Peace. Accept yourself and your circumstances just as they are, remembering that I am sovereign over everything. Do not wear yourself out with analyzing and planning. Instead, let thankfulness and trust be your guides through this day; they will keep you close to Me. As you live in the radiance of My Presence, My Peace shines upon you. You will cease to notice how weak or strong you feel because you will be focusing on Me. The best way to get through this day is step by step with Me. Continue this intimate journey, trusting that the path you are following is headed for heaven.

PSALM 29:11; NUMBERS 6:24–26; PSALM 13:5

The LORD gives

strength

to his people;

the LORD blesses

his people with

peace.

—PSALM 29:11

SEEK MY FACE, and you will find not only My Presence but also My Peace. To receive My Peace, you must change your grasping, controlling stance to one of openness and trust. The only thing you can grasp without damaging your soul is My hand. Ask My Spirit within you to order your day and control your thoughts, for *the mind controlled by the Spirit is Life and Peace.*

You can have as much of Me and My Peace as you want, through thousands of correct choices each day. The most persistent choice you face is whether to trust Me or to worry. You will never run out of things to worry about, but you can choose to trust Me no matter what. I am *an ever-present help in trouble.* Trust Me, *though the earth give way and the mountains fall into the heart of the sea.*

ROMANS 8:6; NUMBERS 6:26 NKJV; PSALM 46:1–2

"The Lord *lift*

up His countenance

upon you, and give

you *peace*."

—Numbers 6:26 NKJV

I AM ABOVE ALL THINGS: your problems, your pain, and the swirling events in this ever-changing world. When you behold My Face, you rise above circumstances and rest with Me in *heavenly realms.* This is the way of Peace, living in the Light of My Presence. I guarantee that you will always have problems in this life, but they must not become your focus. When you feel yourself sinking in the sea of circumstances, say, "*Help me, Jesus!*" and I will draw you back to Me. If you have to say that thousands of times daily, don't be discouraged. I know your weakness, and I meet you in that very place.

EPHESIANS 2:6; MATTHEW 14:28–32; ISAIAH 42:3

"A bruised reed he will not

break, and a smoldering

wick he will not snuff out.

In *faithfulness*

he will bring forth justice."

—Isaiah 42:3

MY PEACE is like a shaft of golden Light shining on you continuously. During days of bright sunshine, it may blend in with your surroundings. On darker days, My Peace stands out in sharp contrast to your circumstances. See times of darkness as opportunities for My Light to shine in transcendent splendor. I am training you to practice Peace that overpowers darkness. Collaborate with Me in this training. *Do not grow weary and lose heart.*

2 THESSALONIANS 3:16;

JOHN 1:4–5 AMP; HEBREWS 12:3

Now may the

Lord of peace himself

give you *peace* at all

times and in every way. The

Lord be with *all* of you.

—2 Thessalonians 3:16

God is our refuge and strength, an ever–present help in trouble. Therefore we will not fear, though the earth give way and the mountains fall into the heart of the sea.

—Psalm 46:1–2

PEACE BE WITH YOU! Ever since the resurrection, this has been My watchword to those who yearn for Me. As you sit quietly, let My Peace settle over you and enfold you in My loving Presence. To provide this radiant Peace for you, I died a criminal's death. Receive *My Peace* abundantly and thankfully. It is a rare treasure, dazzling in delicate beauty, yet strong enough to withstand all onslaughts. Wear My Peace with regal dignity. It will keep your heart and mind close to Mine.

JOHN 20:19, 21; JOHN 14:27; PHILIPPIANS 4:7

On the *evening* of that first day of the week, when the disciples were together, with the doors locked for fear of the Jews, Jesus came and stood *among* them and said, "Peace be with you!" . . . Again Jesus said, "Peace be with you! As the Father has sent me, I am sending you."

—JOHN 20:19, 21

LEARN TO LIVE from your true Center in Me. I reside in the deepest depths of your being, in eternal union with your spirit. It is at this deep level that My Peace reigns continually. You will not find lasting peace in the world around you, in circumstances, or in human relationships. The external world is always in flux—under the curse of death and decay. But there is a gold mine of Peace deep within you, waiting to be tapped. Take time to delve into the riches of My residing Presence. I want you to live increasingly from your real Center, where My Love has an eternal grip on you. *I am Christ in you, the hope of Glory.*

1 THESSALONIANS 5:23;
COLOSSIANS 3:15; COLOSSIANS 1:27

May God himself, the God

of peace, *sanctify*

you through and through.

May your whole spirit,

soul and body be kept

blameless

at the coming of our

Lord Jesus Christ.

—1 THESSALONIANS 5:23

WHEN SOMETHING IN YOUR LIFE OR THOUGHTS makes you anxious, come to Me and talk about it. Bring Me your *prayer and petition with thanksgiving*, saying, "Thank You, Jesus, for this opportunity to trust You more." Though the lessons of trust that I send to you come wrapped in difficulties, the benefits far outweigh the cost.

Well-developed trust will bring you many blessings, not the least of which is My Peace. I have promised to *keep you in perfect Peace* to the extent that you trust in Me. The world has it backward, teaching that peace is the result of having enough money, possessions, insurance, and security systems. *My* Peace, however, is such an all-encompassing gift that it is independent of all circumstances. Though you lose everything else, if you gain My Peace you are rich indeed.

PHILIPPIANS 4:6; ISAIAH 26:3;
2 THESSALONIANS 3:16 NKJV

Do not be

anxious

about anything,

but in everything,

by *prayer*

and petition, with

thanksgiving,

present your requests to God.

—PHILIPPIANS 4:6

I SPEAK TO YOU FROM THE DEPTHS OF YOUR BEING. Hear Me saying soothing words of Peace, assuring you of My Love. Do not listen to voices of accusation, for they are not from Me. I speak to you in love-tones, lifting you up. My Spirit convicts cleanly, without crushing words of shame. Let the Spirit take charge of your mind, combing out tangles of deception. Be transformed by the truth that I live within you.

The Light of My Presence is shining upon you, in benedictions of Peace. Let My Light shine in you; don't dim it with worries or fears. Holiness is letting Me live through you. Since I dwell in you, you are fully equipped to be holy. Pause before responding to people or situations, giving My Spirit space to act through you. Hasty words and actions leave no room for Me; this is atheistic living. I want to inhabit all your moments—gracing your thoughts, words, and behavior.

ROMANS 8:1–2; COLOSSIANS 1:27; 1 CORINTHIANS 6:19

Therefore, there is now no

condemnation

for those who are in Christ

Jesus, because through

Christ Jesus the law of

the *Spirit* of life

set me free from the

law of sin and death.

—ROMANS 8:1-2

STOP TRYING TO WORK THINGS OUT before their times have come. Accept the limitations of living one day at a time. When something comes to your attention, ask Me whether or not it is part of today's agenda. If it isn't, release it into My care and go on about today's duties. When you follow this practice, there will be a beautiful simplicity about your life: *a time for everything, and everything in its time.*

A life lived close to Me is not complicated or cluttered. When your focus is on My Presence, many things that once troubled you lose their power over you. Though the world around you is messy and confusing, remember that *I have overcome the world. I have told you these things, so that in Me you may have Peace.*

ECCLESIASTES 3:1; ECCLESIASTES 8:6–7; JOHN 16:33

There is a *time* for everything, and a *season* for every activity under heaven.

—Ecclesiastes 3:1

And my God will meet all your needs according to his glorious riches in Christ Jesus.

—*Philippians 4:19*

TASTE AND SEE THAT I AM GOOD. The more intimately you experience Me, the more convinced you become of My goodness. I am *the Living One who sees you* and longs to participate in your life. I am training you to find Me in each moment and to be a channel of My loving Presence. Sometimes My blessings come to you in mysterious ways: through pain and trouble. At such times you can know My goodness only through your trust in Me. Understanding will fail you, but trust will keep you close to Me.

Thank Me for the gift of My Peace, a gift of such immense proportions that you cannot fathom its depth or breadth. When I appeared to My disciples after the resurrection, it was Peace that I communicated first of all. I knew this was their deepest need: to calm their fears and clear their minds. I also speak Peace to you, for I know your anxious thoughts. Listen to Me! Tune out other voices so that you can hear Me more clearly. I designed you to dwell in Peace all day, every day. Draw near to Me; receive My Peace.

PSALM 34:8; GENESIS 16:13–14 AMP;
JOHN 20:19; COLOSSIANS 3:15

Let the peace of Christ *rule* in your hearts, since

as members of one body

you were called to peace.
And be *thankful*.

—COLOSSIANS 3:15

I HAVE PROMISED *to meet all your needs according to My glorious riches.* Your deepest, most constant need is for My Peace. I have planted Peace in the garden of your heart, where I live, but there are weeds growing there too: pride, worry, selfishness, unbelief. I am the Gardener, and I am working to rid your heart of those weeds. I do My work in various ways. When you sit quietly with Me, I shine the Light of My Presence directly into your heart. In this heavenly Light, Peace grows abundantly and weeds shrivel up. I also send trials into your life. When you trust Me in the midst of trouble, Peace flourishes and weeds die away. Thank Me for troublesome situations; the Peace they can produce *far outweighs* the trials you endure.

PHILIPPIANS 4:19;

2 THESSALONIANS 3:16 NKJV; 2 CORINTHIANS 4:17

For our light and

momentary troubles are

achieving for

us an eternal glory that

far outweighs them all.

—2 CORINTHIANS 4:17

PEACE IS MY CONTINUAL GIFT TO YOU. It flows abundantly from My throne of grace. Just as the Israelites could not store up manna for the future but had to gather it daily, so it is with My Peace. The day-by-day collecting of manna kept My people aware of their dependence on Me. Similarly, I give you sufficient Peace for the present when you come to me *by prayer and petition with thanksgiving.* If I gave you permanent Peace, independent of My Presence, you might fall into the trap of self-sufficiency. May that never be!

I have designed you to need Me moment by moment. As your awareness of your neediness increases, so does your realization of My abundant sufficiency. *I can meet every one of your needs* without draining My resources at all. *Approach My throne of grace with bold confidence,* receiving My Peace with a thankful heart.

EXODUS 16:15–16, 19;

PHILIPPIANS 4:6–7, 19; HEBREWS 4:16

Let us then approach the

throne of grace

with confidence, so that

we may receive mercy and

find *grace* to help

us in our time of need.

—Hebrews 4:16

DO NOT BE AFRAID, for I am with you. Hear Me saying, *"Peace, be still,"* to your restless heart. No matter what happens, *I will never leave you or forsake you.* Let this assurance soak into your mind and heart until you overflow with Joy. *Though the earth give way and the mountains fall into the heart of the sea*, you need not fear!

The media relentlessly proclaim bad news: for breakfast, lunch, and dinner. A steady diet of their fare will sicken you. Instead of focusing on fickle, ever-changing news broadcasts, tune in to the living Word—the One who is always the same. Let Scripture saturate your mind and heart, and you will walk steadily along the path of Life. Even though you don't know what will happen tomorrow, you can be absolutely sure of your ultimate destination. *I hold you by your right hand, and afterward I will take you into Glory.*

MARK 4:39 NKJV; DEUTERONOMY 31:6;
PSALM 46:2; PSALM 73:23–24

Then He *arose* and

rebuked the wind, and said

to the sea, "Peace, be still!"

And the wind ceased and

there was a great *calm*.

—MARK 4:39 NKJV

DO NOT SEARCH FOR SECURITY in the world you inhabit. You tend to make mental checklists of things you need to do in order to gain control of your life. If only you could check everything off your list, you could relax and be at peace. But the more you work to accomplish that goal, the more things crop up on your list. The harder you try, the more frustrated you become.

There is a better way to find security in this life. Instead of scrutinizing your checklist, focus your attention on My Presence with you. This continual contact with Me will keep you in My Peace. Moreover, I will help you sort out what is important and what is not, what needs to be done now and what does not. *Fix your eyes not on what is seen* (your circumstances), *but on what is unseen* (My Presence).

HEBREWS 3:1; ISAIAH 26:3 NKJV; 2 CORINTHIANS 4:18

You will keep him in

perfect peace,

whose mind is stayed

on You, because he

trusts in You.

—Isaiah 26:3 NKJV

Be strong and courageous. Do not be afraid or terrified because of them, for the LORD your God goes with you; he will never leave you nor forsake you.

—Deuteronomy 31:6

IF YOU LEARN TO TRUST ME—really trust Me—with your whole being, then nothing can separate you from My Peace. Everything you endure can be put to good use by allowing it to train you in trusting Me. This is how you foil the works of evil, growing in grace through the very adversity that was meant to harm you. Joseph was a prime example of this divine reversal, declaring to his brothers: *"You meant evil against me, but God meant it for good."*

Do not fear what this day, or any day, may bring your way. Concentrate on trusting Me and on doing what needs to be done. Relax in My sovereignty, remembering that I go before you, as well as with you, into each day. *Fear no evil*, for I can bring good out of every situation you will ever encounter.

ISAIAH 26:4; GENESIS 50:20 NASB; PSALM 23:4

Trust in the LORD

forever,

for the LORD, the LORD,

is the Rock eternal.

—ISAIAH 26:4

THE PEACE THAT I GIVE YOU transcends your intellect. When most of your mental energy goes into efforts to figure things out, you are unable to receive this glorious gift. I look into your mind and see thoughts spinning round and round: going nowhere, accomplishing nothing. All the while, My Peace hovers over you, searching for a place to land.

Be still in My Presence, inviting Me to control your thoughts. Let My Light soak into your mind and heart until you are aglow with My very Being. This is the most effective way to receive My Peace.

2 THESSALONIANS 3:16; ZECHARIAH 2:13; JOB 22:21

Submit to God and be at

peace with him; in this way

prosperity

will come to you.

—JOB 22:21

Relax in My healing, holy Presence. *Be still* while I transform your heart and mind. *Let go* of cares and worries so that you can receive My Peace. *Cease striving, and know that I am God.*

Do not be like Pharisees who multiplied regulations, creating their own form of "godliness." They got so wrapped up in their own rules that they lost sight of Me. Even today, man-made rules about how to live the Christian life enslave many people. Their focus is on their performance, rather than on Me.

It is through knowing Me intimately that you become like Me. This requires spending time alone with Me. *Let go, relax, be still, and know that I am God.*

Psalm 46:10 nasb; Matthew 23:13; 1 John 3:2

Dear *friends*, now

we are children of God,

and what we will be has

not yet been made known.

But we know that when

he *appears*, we

shall be like him, for we

shall see him as he is.

—1 John 3:2

I WANT TO BE CENTRAL in your entire being. When your focus is firmly on Me, My Peace displaces fears and worries. They will encircle you, seeking entrance, so you must stay alert. Let trust and thankfulness stand guard, turning back fear before it can gain a foothold. *There is no fear in My Love*, which shines on you continually. Sit quietly in My Love-Light while I bless you with radiant Peace. Turn your whole being to trusting and loving Me.

2 THESSALONIANS 3:16; 1 JOHN 4:18;
NUMBERS 6:25–26 NKJV

There is no fear in love. But perfect *love* drives out fear, because fear has to do with punishment. The one who fears is not made *perfect* in love.

—1 John 4:18

Relax in My peaceful Presence. Do not bring performance pressures into our sacred space of communion. When you are with someone you trust completely, you feel free to be yourself. This is one of the joys of true friendship. Though I am *Lord of lords and King of kings*, I also desire to be your intimate Friend. When you are tense or pretentious in our relationship, I feel hurt. I know the worst about you, but I also see the best in you. I long for you to trust Me enough to be fully yourself with Me. When you are real with Me, I am able to bring out the best in you: the very gifts I have planted in your soul. Relax and enjoy our friendship.

2 Thessalonians 3:16 nkjv;
Revelation 17:14; John 15:13–15

They will make war against

the Lamb, but the Lamb

will *overcome*

them because he is Lord

of lords and King of

kings—and with him will

be his called, chosen and

faithful followers.

—REVELATION 17:14

Therefore, since we have been justified through faith, we have peace with God through our Lord Jesus Christ.

—*Romans 5:1*

TRUST ME IN THE DEPTHS of your being. It is there that I live in constant communion with you. When you feel flustered and frazzled on the outside, do not get upset with yourself. You are only human, and the swirl of events going on all around you will sometimes feel overwhelming. Rather than scolding yourself for your humanness, remind yourself that I am both with you and within you.

I am with you at all times, encouraging and supportive rather than condemning. I know that deep within you, where I live, My Peace is your continual experience. Slow down your pace of living for a time. Quiet your mind in My Presence. Then you will be able to hear Me bestowing the resurrection blessing: *Peace be with you*.

COLOSSIANS 1:27; MATTHEW 28:20; JOHN 20:19

"And teaching them to

obey everything I have

commanded

you. And surely I am

with you always, to the

very end of the age."

—Matthew 28:20

UNDERSTANDING WILL NEVER BRING YOU PEACE. That's why I have instructed you to *trust in Me, not in your understanding*. Human beings have a voracious appetite for trying to figure things out in order to gain a sense of mastery over their lives. But the world presents you with an endless series of problems. As soon as you master one set, another pops up to challenge you. The relief you had anticipated is short-lived. Soon your mind is gearing up again: searching for understanding (mastery) instead of seeking Me (your Master).

The wisest of all men, Solomon, could never think his way through to Peace. His vast understanding resulted in feelings of futility, rather than in fulfillment. Finally, he lost his way and succumbed to the will of his wives by worshiping idols.

My Peace is not an elusive goal, hidden at the center of some complicated maze. Actually, you are always enveloped in Peace, which is inherent in My Presence. As you look to Me, you gain awareness of this precious Peace.

PROVERBS 3:5–6; ROMANS 5:1; 2 THESSALONIANS 3:16

Trust in the LORD with all your *heart* and lean not on

your own understanding; in

all your ways acknowledge

him, and he will make your

paths *straight*.

—PROVERBS 3:5-6

TRUST ME in the midst of a messy day. Your inner calm—your Peace in My Presence—need not be shaken by what is going on around you. Though you live in this temporal world, your innermost being is rooted and grounded in eternity. When you start to feel stressed, detach yourself from the disturbances around you. Instead of desperately striving to maintain order and control in your little world, relax and remember that circumstances cannot touch My Peace.

Seek My Face, and I will share My mind with you, opening your eyes to see things from My perspective. *Do not let your heart be troubled, and do not be afraid.* The Peace I give is sufficient for you.

JOHN 16:33; PSALM 105:4; JOHN 14:27

"Peace I leave with you;

my *peace* I give you.

I do not give to you as the

world gives. Do not let your

hearts be troubled

and do not be afraid."

—John 14:27

I AM YOUR BEST FRIEND, as well as your King. Walk hand in hand with Me through your life. Together we will face whatever each day brings: pleasures, hardships, adventures, disappointments. Nothing is wasted when it is shared with Me. *I can bring beauty out of the ashes* of lost dreams. I can glean Joy out of sorrow, Peace out of adversity. Only a Friend who is also the King of kings could accomplish this divine alchemy. There is no other like Me!

The friendship I offer you is practical and down-to-earth, yet it is saturated with heavenly Glory. Living in My Presence means living in two realms simultaneously: the visible world and unseen, eternal reality. I have equipped you to stay conscious of Me while walking along dusty, earthbound paths.

JOHN 15:13–15; ISAIAH 61:3; 2 CORINTHIANS 6:10

And provide for those who grieve in Zion—to bestow on them a crown of *beauty* instead of ashes, the oil of gladness instead of mourning, and a garment of praise instead of a *spirit* of despair. They will be called oaks of righteousness, a planting of the Lord for the display of his splendor.

—Isaiah 61:3

I AM ALWAYS AVAILABLE TO YOU. Once you have trusted Me as your Savior, I never distance Myself from you. Sometimes you may *feel* distant from Me. Recognize that as feeling; do not confuse it with reality. The Bible is full of My promises to be with you always. As I assured Jacob, when he was journeying away from home into unknown places, *I am with you and will watch over you wherever you go.* After My resurrection, I made this promise to My followers: *Surely I am with you always, to the very end of the age.* Let these assurances of My continual Presence fill you with Joy and Peace. No matter what you may lose in this life, you can never lose your relationship with Me.

ISAIAH 54:10; GENESIS 28:15; MATTHEW 28:19–20

"Though the mountains

be shaken and the hills

be removed, yet my

unfailing

love for you will not be

shaken nor my covenant

of peace be removed,"

says the LORD, who has

compassion

on you.

—ISAIAH 54:10

"*I am with you and will watch over you wherever you go, and I will bring you back to this land.*

I will not leave you until I have done what I have promised you."

—*Genesis 28:15*

RECEIVE *MY PEACE*. It is My continual gift to you. The best way to receive this gift is to sit quietly in My Presence, trusting Me in every area of your life. *Quietness and trust* accomplish far more than you can imagine: not only in you, but also on earth and in heaven. When you trust Me in a given area, you release that problem or person into My care.

Spending time alone with Me can be a difficult discipline because it goes against the activity addiction of this age. You may appear to be doing nothing, but actually you are participating in battles going on within spiritual realms. You are waging war—not with *the weapons of the world*, but with heavenly weapons, which *have divine power to demolish strongholds*. Living close to Me is a sure defense against evil.

JOHN 14:27; ISAIAH 30:15; 2 CORINTHIANS 10:4

The weapons we fight with

are not the weapons of the

world. On the contrary, they

have *divine* power

to demolish strongholds.

—2 CORINTHIANS 10:4

YOU WILL NOT FIND MY PEACE by engaging in excessive planning, attempting to control what will happen to you in the future. That is a commonly practiced form of unbelief. When your mind spins with multiple plans, Peace may sometimes seem to be within your grasp; yet it always eludes you. Just when you think you have prepared for all possibilities, something unexpected pops up and throws things into confusion.

I did not design the human mind to figure out the future. That is beyond your capability. I crafted your mind for continual communication with Me. Bring Me all your needs, your hopes and fears. Commit everything into My care. Turn from the path of planning to the path of Peace.

1 PETER 5:6–7; PROVERBS 16:9; PSALM 37:5 NKJV

Humble yourselves,

therefore, under God's mighty

hand, that he may lift you

up in due time. Cast all your

anxiety on him because

he *cares* for you.

—1 PETER 5:6–7

LIVE FIRST AND FOREMOST in My Presence. Gradually you will become more aware of Me than of people and places around you. This awareness will not detract from your relationships with others. Instead, it will increase your ability to give love and encouragement to them. My Peace will permeate your words and demeanor. You will be active in the world, yet one step removed from it. You will not be easily shaken because My enveloping Presence buffers the blow of problems.

This is the path I have set before you. As you follow it wholeheartedly, you experience abundant Life and Peace.

PSALM 89:15–16; PSALM 16:8;
2 PETER 1:2; JOHN 10:28 NKJV

Grace and peace

be yours in

abundance

through the

knowledge

of God and of

Jesus our Lord.

—2 Peter 1:2

BEWARE OF SEEING YOURSELF through other people's eyes. There are several dangers to this practice. First of all, it is nearly impossible to discern what others actually think of you. Moreover, their views of you are variable: subject to each viewer's spiritual, emotional, and physical condition. The major problem with letting others define you is that it borders on idolatry. Your concern to please others dampens your desire to please Me, your Creator.

It is much more real to see yourself through *My eyes*. My gaze upon you is steady and sure, untainted by sin. Through My eyes you can see yourself as one who is deeply, eternally loved. Rest in My loving gaze, and you will receive deep Peace. Respond to My loving Presence by *worshiping Me in spirit and in truth*.

HEBREWS 11:6; ROMANS 5:5; JOHN 4:23–24

And *hope* does not

disappoint us, because God

has poured out his love into

our *hearts* by the Holy

Spirit, whom he has given us.

—ROMANS 5:5

TAKE TIME TO *BE STILL* in My Presence. The more hassled you feel, the more you need this sacred space of communion with Me. Breathe slowly and deeply. Relax in My holy Presence while *My Face shines upon you.* This is how you receive My Peace, which I always proffer to you.

Imagine the pain I feel when My children tie themselves up in anxious knots, ignoring My gift of Peace. I died a criminal's death to secure this blessing for you. Receive it gratefully; hide it in your heart. My Peace is an inner treasure, growing within you as you trust in Me. Therefore, circumstances cannot touch it. Be still, enjoying Peace in My Presence.

PSALM 46:10; NUMBERS 6:25–26; JOHN 14:27

"Be still, and know that

I am God; I will be

exalted

among the nations,

I will be exalted

in the earth."

—Psalm 46:10

Commit your way to the LORD, trust also in Him, and He shall bring it to pass.

—*Psalm 37:5 NKJV*

LIE DOWN IN GREEN PASTURES of Peace. Learn to unwind whenever possible, resting in the Presence of your Shepherd. This electronic age keeps My children "wired" much of the time, too tense to find Me in the midst of their moments. I built into your very being the need for rest. How twisted the world has become when people feel guilty about meeting this basic need! How much time and energy they waste by being always on the go rather than taking time to seek My direction for their lives.

I have called you to walk with Me down *paths of Peace*. I want you to blaze a trail for others who desire to live in My peaceful Presence. I have chosen you less for your strengths than for your weaknesses, which amplify your need for Me. Depend on Me more and more, and I will shower Peace on all your paths.

PSALM 23:1–3; GENESIS 2:2–3; LUKE 1:79

The LORD is my

shepherd,

I shall not be in want. He

makes me lie down in green

pastures, he leads me beside

quiet waters, he restores my

soul. He *guides* me

in paths of righteousness

for his name's sake.

—PSALM 23:1-3

WALK PEACEFULLY WITH ME through this day. You are wondering how you will cope with all that is expected of you. You must traverse this day like any other: one step at a time. Instead of mentally rehearsing how you will do this or that, keep your mind on My Presence and on taking the next step. The more demanding your day, the more help you can expect from Me. This is a training opportunity since I designed you for deep dependence on your Shepherd-King. Challenging times wake you up and amplify your awareness of needing My help.

When you don't know what to do, wait while I open the way before you. Trust that I know what I'm doing, and be ready to follow My lead. *I will give strength to you, and I will bless you with Peace.*

EXODUS 33:14; DEUTERONOMY 33:25;
HEBREWS 13:20–21; PSALM 29:11

The LORD replied, "My

Presence

will go with you, and

I will give you rest."

—EXODUS 33:14

FOCUS YOUR ENTIRE BEING on My living Presence. I am most assuredly with you, enveloping you in My Love and Peace. While you relax in My Presence, I am molding your mind and cleansing your heart. I am re-creating you into the one I designed you to be.

As you move from stillness into the activities of your day, do not relinquish your attentiveness to Me. If something troubles you, talk it over with Me. If you get bored with what you are doing, fill the time with prayers and praise. When someone irritates you, don't let your thoughts linger on that person's faults. Gently nudge your mind back to Me. Every moment is precious if you keep your focus on Me. Any day can be a good day because My Presence permeates all time.

PSALM 89:15–16; 1 JOHN 3:19–20;
JUDE vv. 24–25; PSALM 41:12

In my

integrity

you uphold me

and set me in your

presence

forever.

—Psalm 41:12

AS YOU LOOK at the day before you, you see a twisted, complicated path, with branches going off in all directions. You wonder how you can possibly find your way through that maze. Then you remember the One who is *with you always, holding you by your right hand*. You recall My promise to *guide you with My counsel*, and you begin to relax. As you look again at the path ahead, you notice that a peaceful fog has settled over it, obscuring your view. You can see only a few steps in front of you, so you turn your attention more fully to Me and begin to enjoy My Presence.

The fog is a protection for you, calling you back into the present moment. Although I inhabit all of space and time, you can communicate with Me only here and now. Someday the fog will no longer be necessary, for you will have learned to keep your focus on Me and on the path just ahead of you.

PSALM 73:23–24; PSALM 25:4–5; 1 CORINTHIANS 13:12

Yet I am *always*
with you; you hold me
by my right hand. You
guide me with your
counsel, and afterward
you will take me into glory.

—PSALM 73:23-24

COME TO ME, and rest in My Peace. My Face is shining upon you, in rays of *Peace transcending understanding.* Instead of trying to figure things out yourself, you can relax in the Presence of the One who knows everything. As you lean on Me in trusting dependence, you feel peaceful and complete. This is how I designed you to live: in close communion with Me.

When you are around other people, you tend to cater to their expectations—real or imagined. You feel enslaved to pleasing them, and your awareness of My Presence grows dim. Your efforts to win their approval eventually exhaust you. You offer these people dry crumbs rather than the *living water* of My Spirit flowing through you. This is not My way for you! Stay in touch with Me, even during your busiest moments. Let My Spirit give you words of grace as you live in the Light of My Peace.

PHILIPPIANS 4:6–7; JOHN 7:38; EPHESIANS 5:18–20

"Whoever *believes* in me, as the Scripture has said, streams of *living* water will flow from within him."

—John 7:38

I have set the L<small>ORD</small> always before me. Because he is at my right hand, I will not be shaken.

—*Psalm 16:8*

THANK ME THROUGHOUT THIS DAY for My Presence and My Peace. These are gifts of supernatural proportions. Ever since the resurrection, I have comforted My followers with these messages: *Peace be with you*, and *I am with you always*. Listen as I offer you My Peace and Presence in full measure. The best way to receive these glorious gifts is to thank Me for them.

It is impossible to spend too much time thanking and praising Me. I created you first and foremost to glorify Me. Thanksgiving and praise put you in proper relationship with Me, opening the way for My riches to flow into you. As you thank Me for My Presence and Peace, you appropriate My richest gifts.

LUKE 24:36; MATTHEW 28:20;
HEBREWS 13:15; 2 CORINTHIANS 9:15 NKJV

Through Jesus,

therefore, let us

continually

offer to God a sacrifice

of praise—the fruit

of lips that

confess

his name.

—HEBREWS 13:15

THANK ME FREQUENTLY as you journey through today. This practice makes it possible to *pray without ceasing*, as the apostle Paul taught. If you are serious about learning to pray continually, the best approach is to thank Me in every situation. These thankful prayers provide a solid foundation on which you can build all your other prayers. Moreover, a grateful attitude makes it easier for you to communicate with Me.

When your mind is occupied with thanking Me, you have no time for worrying or complaining. If you practice thankfulness consistently, negative thought patterns will gradually grow weaker and weaker. *Draw near to Me* with a grateful heart, and My Presence will *fill you with Joy and Peace.*

1 THESSALONIANS 5:16–18 KJV;
JAMES 4:8; ROMANS 15:13

May the God of *hope*

fill you with all joy and

peace as you trust in

him, so that you may

overflow with

hope by the power

of the Holy Spirit.

—ROMANS 15:13

LET ME INFUSE MY PEACE into your innermost being. As you sit quietly in the Light of My Presence, you can sense Peace growing within you. This is not something that you accomplish through self-discipline and willpower; it is opening yourself to receive My blessing.

In this age of independence, people find it hard to acknowledge their neediness. However, I have taken you along a path that has highlighted your need for Me, placing you in situations where your strengths were irrelevant and your weaknesses were glaringly evident. Through the aridity of those desert marches, I have drawn you closer and closer to Myself. You have discovered flowers of Peace blossoming in the most desolate places. You have learned to thank Me for hard times and difficult journeys, trusting that through them I accomplish My best work. You have realized that needing Me is the key to knowing Me intimately, which is the gift above all gifts.

JOHN 14:27 NKJV; ISAIAH 58:11; ISAIAH 40:11

"The Lord will *guide* you always; he will satisfy your needs in a sun-scorched land and will *strengthen* your frame. You will be like a well-watered garden, like a spring whose waters never fail."

—Isaiah 58:11

I AM THE *PRINCE OF PEACE.* As I said to My disciples, I say also to you: *Peace be with you.* Since I am your constant Companion, My Peace is steadfastly with you. When you keep your focus on Me, you experience both My Presence and My Peace. Worship Me as King of kings, Lord of lords, and Prince of Peace.

You need My Peace each moment to accomplish My purposes in your life. Sometimes you are tempted to take shortcuts in order to reach your goal as quickly as possible. But if the shortcut requires turning your back on My peaceful Presence, you must choose the longer route. Walk with Me along paths of Peace; enjoy the journey in My Presence.

ISAIAH 9:6; JOHN 20:19–21; PSALM 25:4 NKJV

For to us a child is *born*,

to us a son is given, and

the government will be on

his *shoulders*.

And he will be called

Wonderful Counselor,

Mighty God, Everlasting

Father, Prince of Peace.

—Isaiah 9:6

REST IN ME, MY CHILD, forgetting about the worries of the world. Focus on Me—Immanuel—and let My living Presence envelop you in Peace. Tune in to My eternal security, for *I am the same yesterday, today, and forever.* If you live on the surface of life by focusing on ever-changing phenomena, you will find yourself echoing the words of Solomon: *"Meaningless! Meaningless! Everything is meaningless!"*

Living in collaboration with Me is the way to instill meaning into your days. Begin each day alone with Me so that you can experience the reality of My Presence. As you spend time with Me, the way before you opens up step by step. Arise from the stillness of our communion, and gradually begin your journey through the day. Hold My hand in deliberate dependence on Me, and I will smooth out the path before you.

MATTHEW 1:22–23; HEBREWS 13:8;
ECCLESIASTES 1:2; PROVERBS 3:6

Jesus Christ

is the

same

yesterday and today

and forever.

—HEBREWS 13:8

"And I give them eternal life,
and they shall never perish;
neither shall anyone snatch
them out of My hand."

—John 10:28 *NKJV*

I AM SPEAKING in the depths of your being. Be still so that you can hear My voice. I speak in the language of Love; My words fill you with Life and Peace, Joy and Hope. I desire to talk with all of My children, but many are too busy to listen. The "work ethic" has them tied up in knots. They submit wholeheartedly to this taskmaster, wondering why they feel so distant from Me.

Living close to Me requires making Me your *First Love*—your highest priority. As you seek My Presence above all else, you experience Peace and Joy in full measure. I also am blessed when you make Me first in your life. While you journey through life in My Presence, *My Glory brightens the world around you.*

PSALM 119:64; ISAIAH 50:4;
REVELATION 2:4; ISAIAH 60:2

The Sovereign Lord has given

me an instructed tongue, to

know the word that

sustains the weary. He wakens

me morning by morning,

wakens my ear to

listen like one being taught.

—Isaiah 50:4

DO NOT BE WEIGHED DOWN by the clutter in your life: lots of little chores to do sometime, in no particular order. If you focus too much on these petty tasks, trying to get them all out of the way, you will discover that they are endless. They can eat up as much time as you devote to them.

Instead of trying to do all your chores at once, choose the ones that need to be done today. Let the rest slip into the background of your mind so I can be in the forefront of your awareness. Remember that your ultimate goal is living close to Me, being responsive to My initiatives. I can communicate with you most readily when your mind is uncluttered and turned toward Me. Seek My Face continually throughout this day. Let My Presence bring order to your thoughts, infusing Peace into your entire being.

PROVERBS 16:3; MATTHEW 6:33;
PSALM 27:8 NKJV; ISAIAH 26:3 NKJV

"But *seek* first

his kingdom and

his righteousness, and

all these things will be

given to you as well."

—Matthew 6:33

I SPEAK TO YOU from the depths of eternity. *Before the world was formed, I AM!* You hear Me in the depths of your being, where I have taken up residence. *I am Christ in you, the hope of Glory.* I, your Lord and Savior, am alive within you. Learn to tune in to My living Presence by seeking Me in silence.

As you celebrate the wonder of My birth in Bethlehem, celebrate also your rebirth into eternal life. This everlasting gift was the sole purpose of My entering your sin-stained world. Receive My gift with awe and humility. Take time to explore the vast dimensions of My Love. Allow thankfulness to flow freely from your heart in response to My glorious gift. *Let My Peace rule in your heart, and be thankful.*

PSALM 90:2 AMP; COLOSSIANS 1:27;
JOHN 3:3; COLOSSIANS 3:15

To them God has

chosen to make

known among the Gentiles

the glorious riches of

this *mystery*,

which is Christ in you,

the hope of glory.

—Colossians 1:27

RECEIVE MY PEACE. This is still your deepest need, and I, your *Prince of Peace*, long to pour Myself into your neediness. My abundance and your emptiness are a perfect match. I designed you to have no sufficiency of your own. I created you as a *jar of clay*, set apart for sacred use. I want you to be filled with My very Being, permeated through and through with Peace.

Thank Me for My peaceful Presence, regardless of your feelings. Whisper My Name in loving tenderness. *My Peace*, which lives continually in your spirit, will gradually work its way through your entire being.

ISAIAH 9:6; 2 CORINTHIANS 4:7; JOHN 14:26–27

But we have this

treasure in jars of clay

to show that this

all-surpassing

power is from

God and not from us.

—2 Corinthians 4:7

COME TO ME WITH A THANKFUL HEART so that you can enjoy My Presence. This is the day that I have made. I want you to rejoice *today*, refusing to worry about tomorrow. Search for all that I have prepared for you, anticipating abundant blessings and accepting difficulties as they come. I can weave miracles into the most mundane day if you keep your focus on Me.

Come to Me with all your needs, knowing that *My glorious riches* are a more-than-adequate supply. Stay in continual communication with Me so that you can live above your circumstances even while you are in the midst of them. *Present your requests to Me with thanksgiving, and My Peace, which surpasses all comprehension, will guard your heart and mind.*

PSALM 118:24; PHILIPPIANS 4:19;
PHILIPPIANS 4:6–7 NASB

This is the day

the Lord has made;

let us

rejoice

and be

glad in it.

—Psalm 118:24

He tends his flock like a shepherd:
He gathers the lambs in his
arms and carries them close
to his heart; he gently leads
those that have young.

—Isaiah 40:11